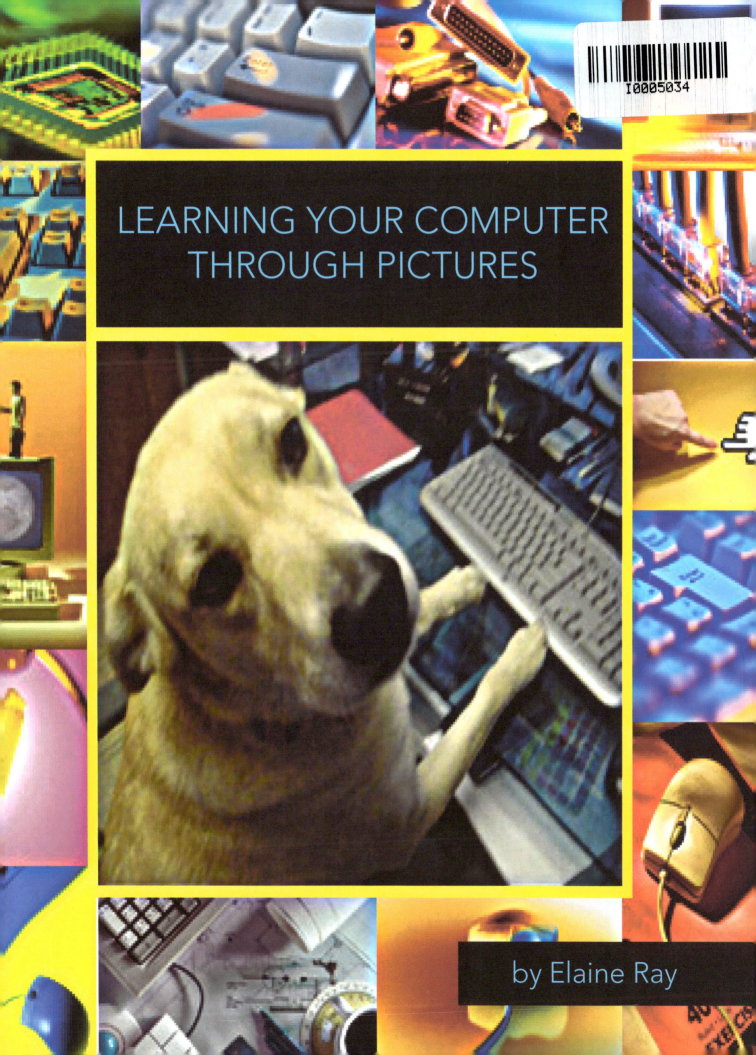

LEARNING YOUR COMPUTER THROUGH PICTURES

by Elaine Ray

Learning Your Computer Through Pictures

§§

This book is designed to give you the basics in understanding and using your computer. The format is simple and all of the instructions are coupled with pictorial examples which will take away any apprehension you may have as each instruction is supported with its correlating picture every step of the way.

Testimonial from a Student of This Book:

I am really amazed by the book, "Learning Your Computer Through Pictures." I can't find the words to express my impressions of this Author's self teaching computers' textbook. This book is the easiest, simplest, and the clearest self-teaching textbook pertaining to computers that I have ever studied.

This really is helpful for people of my age group who didn't get a chance to study this subject in a formal classroom while in college. I have college degrees, was one of those outstanding community leaders, am considered to be a very smart and hard working woman by my peers; but, because of the frustration I have experienced due to my lack of computer knowledge, I have lost so many opportunities and positions.

I couldn't attend computer class, because, I was ashamed to sit with the young students which are my children's age that know more than I do about computers. Thanks to Elaine Ray's self teaching text book, in two days, I gained a lot of computer knowledge which I hadn't dreamed I would have attained in my entire life time.

I recommend this book to everyone like myself, who are of the older generation; and perhaps come from another country, to use this text book's instructions to help them to live their lives with confidence in this modern world.

Almaz Mekonen
Columbus, Ohio

You may also purchase a hard copy of this book by visiting my website at:
www.theundefeatedlifet-shirts.com

Introduction:

Why is this Dog Sleeping?

This book is designed to provide you with the basics in understanding computer operations through pictorial instructions that will help you to feel confident as you share your insights and ideas through your computer, and online.

Today, we are living in a computer age. With our computers we have the unique opportunity to express ourselves throughout the world; however many people feel apprehensive when trying to learn the operations of their computers, perceiving computers as too complicated to understand.

In my online interactions with people, I realized that many people have valuable insights, or wonderful things to talk about; though many simply do not know how to use their computers the way they would like in order to share their ideas with others online.

Because of this, I decided to write this book, "Learning Your Computer Through Pictures". This book is designed to give you the basics in understanding and using your computer. The format is simple and all of the instructions are coupled with pictorial examples which will take away any apprehension you may have as each instruction is supported with its correlating picture every step of the way.

We will cover things like the creation of documents, how to share those documents online, the operational features of the Microsoft Works word processing program, creation of video formats, navigating on the web, and insightful little tips to make things easier as you explore your computer applications.

In many instances, the best way to learn something is to see it being done and then actually do it yourself by following examples. Experience is the best teacher right? Well as you go through this tutorial and practice at home on your own computer you will easily find that, *YOU CAN DO IT! AND, IT IS FUN TOO!*

It is fun to learn new things, especially when you are learning things which add to your own creative desires and abilities. That is what I want to help you with in creating this book for you. This book will be fun to work with as it easily displays each step you need to follow as you create your own documents and videos, explore the applications of your program files, and navigate the internet.

I have included a Vocabulary Terms page just after the index to help you understand some of the terms as you come across them in studying this book. Congratulations to you! When you finish the studies of this book you will have a great starting point in your computer and online journey.

This book is dedicated to the desire for self expression that resides in all of us.

Thank you,
Elaine Ray
TheUndefeatedLife

Table of Contents

Table of Contents

Table of Contents

Table of Contents

Vocabulary Terms

[A]

A Hard Drive is a ROM: A "Read Only Memory" disk within your computer's hardware. It contains Read Only Memory, e.g. program commands that allow your computer to operate within the parameters of both your "OS" System...operating system, and the other various program applications that you will be using as you get to know your computer's operational functions.

Audio/Music Timeline: This is the parameter location designated within the Movie Maker's story board workspace. It designates when audio will start and stop. Audio tracks can be manipulated with variable start and stop run times from within the time line parameter itself within the time line application.

[B]

Book Marking Your Favorite Sites: Just as when you are reading a book, and want to save the page location so you can come back to it; the internet provides this same type of application with the Book Mark, or Favorites' Feature. Bookmarks or Favorites' store your internet sites in a folder named the same depending on your internet provider.

[C]

Control Panel: The Control Panel allows you to create specific operational settings on your computer. You can modify your desktop's appearance, perform maintenance functions, set up your internet specifications, and much more.

Cursor: The cursor is the visual representation of where your mouse arrow is positioned within a document, or window. It is usually viewed as a small vertical line that appears to be blinking.

[D]

Desk Top: In computer terms, the desktop is the first window that comes up when you turn your computer. On you desk top you will see various program icons that are called "Short Cuts" that allow you to open and begin using a particular program.

Dragging, or Drag: This usually pertains to a computer application within a program; for instance, as when dragging a picture to the story board, or as when dragging your mouse over text to highlight that area.

Download: A down load pertains to removing information from another source, either online or within a program file. You are taking information from one location and downloading it to another location within your computer files.

Drop Down Menus: These are menus that appear when you click on one of the functions of your word processing program; or within various online software applications.

Vocabulary Terms

[E]

Edit Tab: This is a drop down menu option found within many tool bar applications, whether online, or in a document's tool bar application.

[F]

File Name: A file name is a search parameter. When you save a file by giving it a name in this parameter, you are designating the file's name as your computer's search parameter.

Font Color Tab: This tab is found within your MS Word program. This is a program application that allows you to change the text color when working within a document.

Format: This usually refers to a Page Setup feature; or how you will display a picture placed within a document.

[H]

Hyper-Link: A hyper-link is usually an internet website location, or address. So for example, if you wanted someone to be able to click on a picture of a product you have posted on your website, and with that click, be taken to the shopping cart to purchase that item, you would need to insert the hyper-link location for that item's shopping cart location from the appropriate website address.

[I]

Import Pictures: This is a program application that prompts you to upload pictures from a file location and place them in another location such as within a document, within a slide show, or any other location that supports the operations of this application. When you use this function, an "Insert File" window pops up, allowing you to incorporate a selected picture into your "Import File Window Application".

[K]

Key Words and Meta Tags: These are content specific words that you use to describe the document or product that you are representing to search engines. When you use these key words, they in fact become search specific words that the internet uses to find information related to specific search engine criteria. So if I want to promote my book I would enter the title of the book, and other key words such as learning computers, creating videos, uploading videos, and teaching computer operations. Then, when someone types a search using on of these words, my material will appear on the search results page.

[L]

Line in/Mic in: This pertains to your computer's internal microphone.
You can use your computer's internal microphone system to record your voice onto your video presentations. Most web cameras record both video and audio, and their line in microphones are of a better quality that your computer's line in microphone; so you may want to set an alternate microphone system as your computer's default line in microphone.

Vocabulary Terms

[L]

Link: A link in computer terminology refers to a location found either online or within a file location that contains specific information. Usually, an online link is the landing page for either a website, or specific information.

[M]

Microsoft Clip Art: This is an internal extension to the MS Word program's graphics application program files. In other words if you click on the "Clip art on Office Online" you will be taken to this web address http://office.microsoft.com/en-us/images/ where you can download graphics online.

Microsoft Works Program: This is a computerized word processing program commonly installed on most manufactured computers, regardless of the make of the computer.

[N]

Note Pad Program Application: The Note Pad is a program application found within your computer's OS System, "Operating System" that serves as a document transference application allowing you to transfer coded text type documents into a simple, un-coded text format. The Note Pad creates and edits text documents using basic formatting.

[O]

OS System = Operating System: The OS System is your computer's operating system. The OS is a set of computer program commands which tell your computer how to operate within specific program applications.   Windows is one of the most commonly known operating systems.

[P]

Page Setup: This is a MS Works program application which allows you to format your document page specifications.

Picture Toolbar: This is your graphics editing tool. With this toolbar you can, format the picture, adjust the light and contrast, format a boarder, set the layout of the picture, adjust the size, and set the hues and color saturation levels.

Pop Up Application (or Window): A Pop Up Application is a feature of a program, a program application's functions, such as a sign on screen, or it can also be a tool bar, such as with the picture toolbar when working with graphics.

Program Application: This is an application function such as saving files, converting files, editing information, and basically any function within a program that allows the program to perform its purpose.

Vocabulary Terms

[R]

RAM, "Random Access Memory": This is your computer's storage program application memory. When you pull up various program functions, RAM is in use and telling your OS system about the program application so that a particular program will be initiated.

Refresh Button: This is a button found on internet toolbars which allows you to refresh/restore the current page you are on if, for example, that page stops working properly. Also, if the internet pages have added new content since the last time you visited, by pressing the refresh button you will see any new content.

Right Click: This pertains to the right button on your mouse which is designed to perform those "right click" functions designated within your computer's operating system.

[S]

Scroll Bar: This a slide bar tool, seen usually on the right, within a computer application's window that lets you move the page you are viewing up and down to scroll through the contents of a window you are viewing, a file location, a open file's contents themselves, or within a document.

Select All: This is a program application and exists as a drop down menu application. This feature allows you to block out a group of text, and by right clicking again on the highlighted text area, another menu is generated with the prompt of copy, cut, paste, and so on.

Setting the Font: This means that you are selecting what type of text you would like displayed as you type your document.

[T]

Text Animation: This is another program application of the MS Movie Maker program. This feature allows your text to fade in and out, appear and disappear, type in one letter at a time, and so on. These types of animation add greater entertainment to your movie.

[U]

Upload: An upload basically performs the same function, except that an upload can come from a third party site or shared file location.

URL: This is a Universal Recognized Location or landing page for a website. It is also known as a web address.

[V]

Video Durations: Durations pertains to the amount of "play time" that each slide will run with as presented in the slideshow while the video presentation is in its "play mode."

Vocabulary Terms

[V]

Video Effects: This is a visual effect that can add dramatically to, and enhance the presentation of your video slideshow. You can fade in a picture, make it spiral in or out, make it appear as an old film, brighten or darken each slide as it appears, or you can have each slide pan to the right or left which gives a slide a sense that it is moving.

Video File: Within computer concepts, a video file can be two things. It can be your computer's default file folder on your hard drive where your videos are automatically stored unless you designate a different file location during the save process; or, it can be a Video itself that you had initially created as a slide show that will be converted into video format and saved as a video file during the save process.

Video Transitions: Between each individual slide of a video slide show presentation is a space that is designed to allow for a transitional effect to occur between the slides. These transitions enhance the viewer's perceptions of your video. They can be things like fading from one slide to another, or spiraling out and into the next slide. These are fun little attractions that you can incorporate into your overall presentation.

[W]

Window: A window is the opened viewing area of your computer and its applications. Windows can be pop-up menu applications, or additional work areas created within an already opened application field; example, as when creating a text box within an already opened document.

Windows®: This is the name of the Microsoft Operating System. Today's most common Windows OS system is either Windows XP, or Windows Vista.

How to Create a Microsoft Word Document

First you must have a Microsoft Works Program; I am using Microsoft Office Student and Teacher Edition 2003…. This is an older version; however the basic document creation functions remain the same so let's get started o.k.?

First you need to click on the start **start** button found on the lower left of your computer screen.

From there, you can do one of two things to access your MS Works word processing program.

Here are your choices…

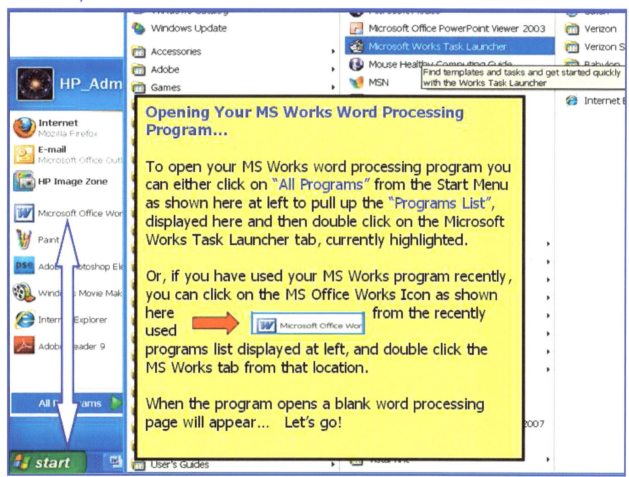

So now you have opened up the word processing program through one of the options listed above and you want to create a document. I always like to format my page prior to starting to type in the document field.

Go to the next page for information on how to format your document page.

How to Format Your Document Page

Formatting Your Document...

O.K. first, with your blank page in view, you look to the top left of your word processing screen as shown here at left and click "File" and hold down the mouse long enough for the drop down menu to appear as shown here.   Then you click on "Page Setup" from that menu application.

When you click on page setup, a pop up window appears as shown below at right. At this point you need to set up your page margins, so click on the "Margins" tab as shown now.

Setting up the Margins...
On this menu you use your mouse and the up and down arrows to enlarge the page margins with the up arrow, or decrease the page margins with the down arrows.

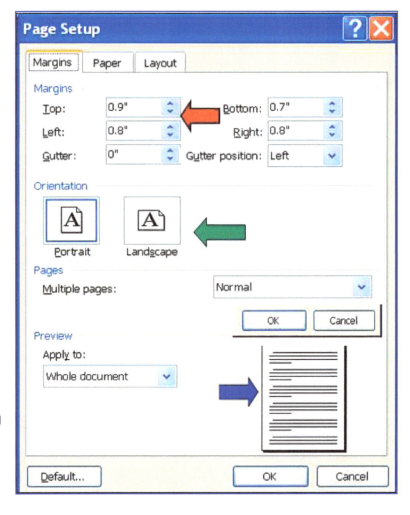

Note: you will need to adjust the top, bottom, left, and right side margins. You will see how the changes appear in the page icon pointed out with the blue arrow.

You will also need to decide whether you want your page displayed in a portrait or landscape format by clicking on your choice as indicated with the green arrow.

O.K., that is the basics to get you started. Be sure to click on the OK button when you are done to save your changes.   If you don't like what you have done click cancel and start over.

Now it is time to select the font you want your document to be typed in, Let's Go!

How to Select a Font for Your Document & Open Your Saved Pictures Files

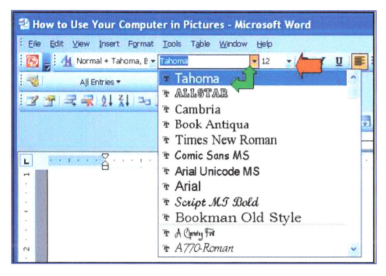

O.K., now you are ready to set the font you like into your document. "Setting the Font" means that you are selecting what type of text you would like displayed as you type your document. To do that you click on the second whitened window shown here at left, and click on the drop down arrow, indicated with a green arrow. You will find this view at the top and left side of your document page. The red arrow at left shows you that you need to click on each of the "down arrows" to access the drop down menus that display the various fonts to select from, and then the size that you want your font to be. I have highlighted "Tahoma" and clicked on its name so that my text will be displayed in The Tahoma Font.

By clicking on the drop down arrow to the right of the Font selection window as shown here at right (red arrow), you can now select the size of font you want to use. I have selected font size 12 by clicking on the number 12 so that the window closes and that font is now in place. Now you are ready to start typing…..but wait! Let's say you want to insert a picture into your document to attract interest, or to display what you are talking about. Here's how to do that.

Adding Pictures: Opening Your Pictures Storage File on Your Computer

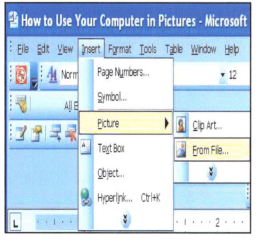

Here we are… With your cursor "the mouse arrow" blinking **within** the page of the document, decide where you want to insert a picture and place your cursor there. Then as pictured to the left, click on insert so that the drop down menu appears, click picture so that another parallel drop down menu appears and make a selection from either file, to access a picture stored on your hard drive in your Pictures Files; or you can select from Microsoft Clip Art online, which is an application feature of your MS Word Program, in order to access the many clip art pictures available to you there.

Opening Your Pictures Storage File on Your Computer

Adding Pictures (continued):

First let's go through the steps to insert a picture from your picture files on your computer's hard drive. A hard drive is a ROM, "Read Only Memory" disk within your computer's hardware. It contains Read Only Memory, e.g. program commands that allow your computer to operate within the parameters of both your "OS" System...operating system, and the other various program applications that you will be using as you get to know your computer's operational functions. RAM, "Random Access Memory" is your computer's storage program application memory. When you pull up various program functions and applications, RAM is in use and telling your OS about the program application so that a particular program will be initiated.

Finding Pictures Inside Your Computer's Picture Folder

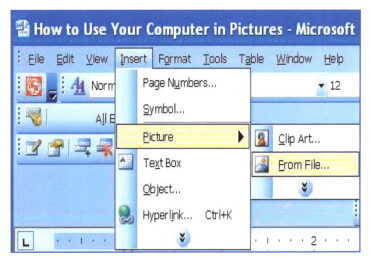

O.K., let's get started inserting a picture from your computer's saved pictures folder. As stated before, with your cursor "the mouse arrow" blinking within the page of the document, decide where you want to insert a picture and place your cursor there. Then as pictured to the left click on insert so that the drop down menu appears, click picture so that another parallel drop down menu appears and make a selection From File...

This is what happens next...

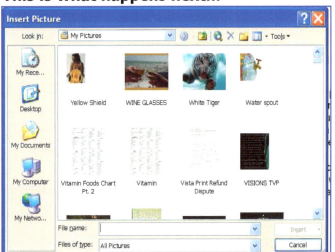

You will then generate a new pop-up window containing your complete pictures files. Let's explore the options here.

In your pictures file, you will have pictures saved in your general pictures files as shown here at left and you will also have some pictures which you have saved in a "Named Folder" of picture projects you may want to save for either work or enjoyment. I'll explain as we go on.

Finding Pictures Inside Your Computer's Picture Folder, (continued)

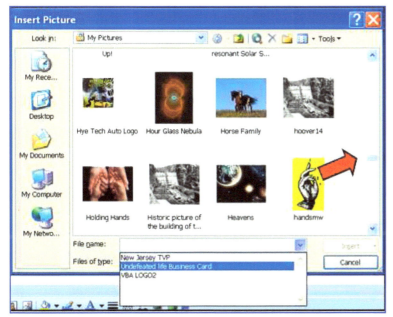

To see all of the pictures stored in your general pictures file, and with the picture window open as shown here, you need to use the scroll bar "indicated with the red arrow" to move up and down through your picture file to make a selection. If you remember the name of the picture you are looking for you can simply type that name in the file name section as shown at bottom to bring up a drop down menu of recently used and saved pictures. Now let's look at finding pictures stored in file folders within your computer's general pictures file.

Finding Pictures Stored in Your Computer's Pictures File, Inside a Separately Named Picture File Folder...

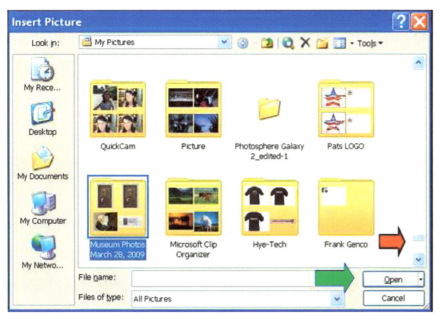

Welcome Back! I hope you are enjoying this as you play around with getting to know your computer functions in a word processing document.

As you know, we talked about how some of your pictures are stored in your general pictures file as individual pictures. There are also pictures which you may have created a file folder for within your pictures file. Sometimes these files appear at the beginning of the picture file, and sometimes they are at the end as mine are here. If your picture files are not on the top of your picture file stored under "My Pictures", then use your scroll bar shown here to the right, (red arrow) to scroll down and see your picture folders. Note we will learn how to create a folder, and name it for your particular needs in the next section. As shown above, I have found my picture folder titled "Museum Photos, March 28, 2009". To access these pictures I highlight the folder by clicking on it and then click "Open", indicated with the (green arrow) to view the objects in the selected file folder.

Finding Pictures Stored in Your Computer's Pictures File, Inside a Separately Named Picture File Folder, (continued)...

Here is what happens next...

I have clicked on my Museum Photos and with that click, a new window has opened showing me the pictures in that file. The (red arrow) shows what file folder I am looking in.

So I have highlighted my selected picture, and now I need to click on the "Insert Button" as indicated with the (green arrow) to insert the picture.

Here is my picture...

Note, this picture was very large and I had to re-size it so that it fits in this space. Let's go on to...

How to Re-Size a Picture

When I originally inserted the eagle picture shown above, this is how large it actually was...

So now let's go through the steps to resize this picture. There are two ways to do this in a simple context.

First, notice the little squares at each of the corners and in the middle of this picture as indicated with (red arrows). When an inserted picture

comes up at first in the document, as this picture, it will be what ever size it was saved as originally; it will not have these corner markers showing. To reveal these markers simply click on the picture once and two things will happen.

How to Re-Size a Picture, (continued)...

First, as shown on the previous page, the corner markers will appear, and secondly you will see the "Picture Toolbar" shown at right. This is a "Pop Up Application".

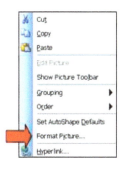

Using the Picture Toolbar to Edit a Picture...
The picture tool bar, shown at right, is the second way to edit your picture attributes. But if you just want a quick re-size of the picture you can click on the corner markers to adjust the size of the picture as explained on the previous page. If you want the picture to remain in the same proportions and just get smaller, place your mouse over one of the <u>corner markers</u> and when you see a diagonal arrow appear just hold down your left mouse button and slide your mouse to the inside of the picture at the diagonal to decrease the size. You can also make a picture narrower by doing the same with the side markers, and you can also enlarge the picture in the same fashion.

You can bring up this tool bar, shown above, by right clicking with your mouse while your mouse is placed in the picture field. The menu activated when you "right click" in the picture field will look like this. From here you select, "Format Picture."

Formatting a Picture Using the Picture Toolbar

O.K. remember the easiest way to bring up your picture toolbar is to right click on your mouse's right button while the mouse is placed within the picture. Then you select format picture to bring up the following "Format Picture Window" with its tabs. Here is how that menu pop-up looks like as shown below - (1).

(1)

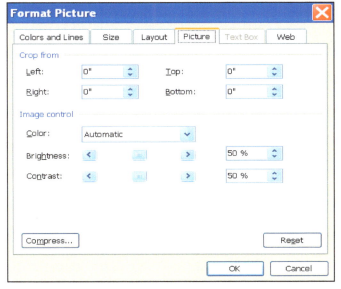

When you first pull this menu up, you will see the "Picture Tab" highlighted as shown at left. Here you can adjust the size, brightness, contrast, and other features of the picture appearance itself. If you want to frame your picture with a line, click on the "Colors and Lines" tab. Then you will see the menu shown on the next page – (2).

Formatting a Picture Using the Picture Toolbar, (continued)...

(2)

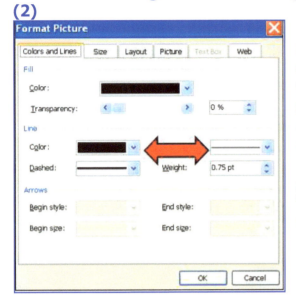

Here you can change the line color by clicking on the drop down arrow of the Line Color drop down arrow; you can also change the Line Thickness by using the drop down arrow shown here to the right of the line color. These options are indicated with the (red arrow).

Another option in the "Format Picture Menu" is the "Layout Tab Menu Box", shown here at lower right. Here you can set the positioning of the picture.

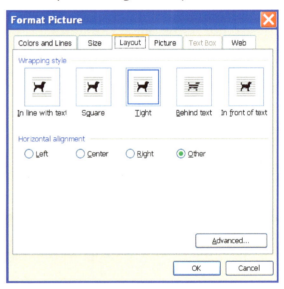

Tight = To have the text wrap around the picture.
In Line w/Text = Creates a space across the page where the picture is.
Square = Text is tightly wrapped around the picture in a square frame.
Behind Text = Text types through the picture; the picture can be lightened so that it appears as a watermark.
In Front of Text = Picture is super-imposed over the text.

Those are the basics in working with pictures.

Creating an Additional Picture File Folder within Your Stored Pictures

O.K. first you have inserted a picture into your document, and let's say you want to save that picture into a separate file that targets the use for which you may want to attain that picture again such as my picture here of the dog sleeping.

Why is this Dog Sleeping?

O.K., I know that as I continue to type this book I will be using pictures of this dog sleeping throughout my document. Because of this, I would like to save it in a file so I can get to it easily, without having to search through my entire picture files and folders. I can save it in its own file for easy retrieval, here's how.

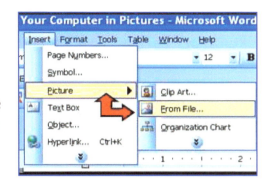

First I need to open my pictures file, I can do this easily by clicking on Insert, Picture, from File as shown here:

Now while in the picture file folder, having performed the steps shown here at right, then, at the top of the picture file's tool bar I need to click on create new file as shown here below.

When I click on "Create New Folder", I get this pop-up window. Here I type in the name of the new folder and click OK. After clicking on "O.K.," I will see my file folder open up and I can now save my pictures of the Dog Sleeping in this file for easy access.

Here is my new file folder as seen within my "Stored Pictures Files." In the future, I can find my dog pictures easily by clicking on the file folder verses having to scroll through all the pictures of dogs from within my picture files, now I can simply access the "Sleeping Dog Pictures" from my created "Why is this Dog Sleeping" folder.

Let's move on to creating hyper-links into your documents and pictures.

Creating Hyper-Links Into Words Within Your Document...

What is a Hyper-Link? A hyper-link is usually an internet website location, or address. So for example, if you wanted someone to be able to click on a picture of a product you have posted on your website, and with that click, be taken to the shopping cart to purchase that item, you would need to insert the hyper-link location for that item's shopping cart location from the appropriate website address. O.K., now let's talk about inserting hyper-links into the text portion of your document.

Creating Hyper-Links into Words Within Your Document, (continued)...

Here is my example; I am going to insert a hyper-link into the words Hubble Telescope:

Example: "Did you know that the Hubble Telescope rotates in a fixed orbit around the planet earth?"

After typing the word or words you want to become a hyper-link, you then highlight the words as shown here by holding down the left mouse button and then dragging the mouse over the words so that they appear as this:

that the **Hubble Telescope** rotates

Now you go to the top of your document page and click on "Insert", and then select "Hyper-link" as shown here. After I click Hyperlink from the drop down menu, a new window opens up that allows me to type in the URL "website location" and insert it as a hyper-link.

Here is how that window looks...

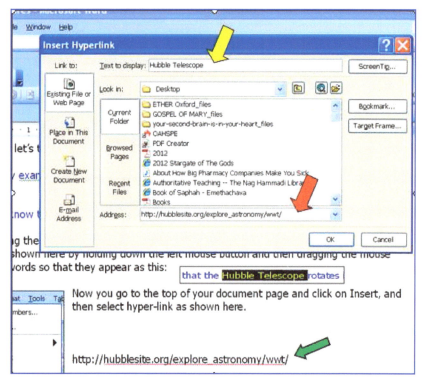

Notice that yellow arrow? That identifies the text to display as a platform for the hyper-link, and you can see that the words are Hubble Telescope, as I had them highlighted before clicking on insert hyper-link as described above.

At the bottom, identified with a red arrow is the word "address" this is where I need to type in the hyper-link to the site information on the Hubble Telescope.

Here's a Tip!

Sometimes you cannot simply copy and paste in your website address, having visited the site prior to inserting the hyper-link. I usually copy the website address and temporarily paste it where I can see it within the document as shown with the green arrow so that I can type it in correctly. After typing in your website address, be sure to click on OK to save your hyper-link setting.

When you have successfully inserted a hyper-link into a word, and you move your mouse over that word, you will see a hyper-link window identifier pop-up showing the hyper-link URL that looks like this.

When you move your mouse over the word or words and see this, you know your hyper-link is inserted into the word or words properly as designated.

Inserting Hyper-Links into your Pictures...

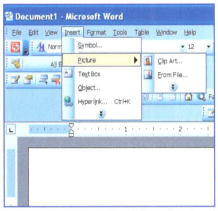

1) First, open your document, then, place your mouse over insert to get the displayed drop down menu.
Now click on picture and move your mouse over to either from file, if you want to insert a picture from your pictures file folder, or Clip Art; which will take you to Microsoft Office Online as displayed here at right. With this application, you type the name of the picture you are looking for in the "Search for:" window and click the green arrow.

If you do not see the picture you want in the MS Word's directory of Microsoft graphics; you can click on the Microsoft Online tab as shown at right. This is an online product application of your MS Word Program which has a free picture download gallery from which you can upload pictures and store them in your picture files folder.

2) Clicking on "File" will take you to the stored picture folder which is on your computer's hard drive. Once you have selected the picture you want to insert into your document by clicking on it once to highlight it as shown at left (red arrow), then click on the insert tab to bring that picture into your document.

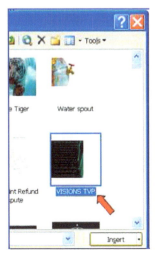

3) Once you have selected your picture and clicked insert, that picture will appear in the current document your working in.

4) When I click on the picture, two things happen as shown here at right. First the picture is framed in bubbles, and secondly the picture tool bar appears as
now shown below the picture of the tiger at right.

Here is my Picture:

How to Create a Video Slide Show with Microsoft Movie Maker
Part Sixteen

Converting Your Slide Show into a Movie File... Let's Go!

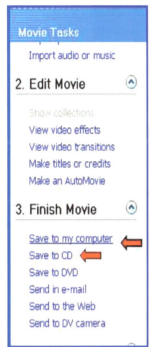

We have come so far now. I hope this has been as fun for you as it has been for me to bring you to this point. Now that we have created our slide show movie, have added the music audio file, and our narration, its time to save the movie. Let's get to it so we can see our final take.

O.K. the first step is to click on "Save to my computer", (shown at left), so that you can upload it in the future from your computer. When you click on this option you will see the next window that pops up as shown here at right. In this window you need to name your video by typing that name into the field identified with the number 1, (1st yellow arrow).

Note, I have already saved this file while in Microsoft Movie Maker program, and the name I gave it is the name currently displayed in field number one.

It is a good idea to re-name the final movie project so that you can go back and use the initial story board project as the framework for another movie.

You will also see the second field identified with, (2), designates where my video file will be saved. The default setting in Windows is "My Videos." If you want to save it somewhere else click on the browse button to access a drop down menu of alternate locations as displayed in the inset at right. To designate a different file location to save your finished movie, simply click on the "save to" location which you will see when the "Browse for Folder" window is closed, and then click on **OK** to save to that file location.

Now, when you have finished making these selections with regard to saving your movie by completing the options as displayed in the menus above, you simply click on the "Next" button to proceed with the process.

Converting Your Slide Show into a Movie File... (Continued)

On the previous page we named our movie, selected the file location that we wanted to save our movie to, and then we clicked on the "Next" button.   That brought up the menu window displayed here at right. This is your "Save Movie Wizard", a MS Movie Maker program application. Let's look at our options here within this menu's function. You will see that the default setting, as indicated is, "Best quality for playback on my computer (recommended)".

The yellow arrow shows a heading of, <u>Show fewer choices</u>... If you click on this option, what will be displayed is only the option of "Best Quality" as shown at the top of the list. I would say that the "Recommended

Settings" options are always the best to follow for the new person who is just starting out making computerized movie formats. The rest of the settings you see in this window are staying in line with the recommended settings; and for the basic computer user, you are good to go with these settings. So having affirmed these are the settings you want for your movie, you then click on the "Next" button to proceed.

This is your Root Directory Video File's Location.

Having clicked the "Next Button", the next window displayed is shown here at left. You can see that your movie is in production at 2% completed, that it is being saved with your specific <u>Movie File Name</u>, and that the "Save To" destination folder is \My Videos\.

Note that the **Root Directory follows the "C" prompt, e.g. C:\ as seen here under Destination.   The "C" prompt is your computer's hard drive.**

The full line of text that you see displayed here is called the destination path. Also note that even though you saved this movie file within your "My Videos" folder the default and root directory is always "Documents and Settings."

When you open up your documents folder and scroll

There is nothing more to do now other than wait for your movie to finish the saving process. Sit back and relax, you have accomplished a lot here...congrats!

Accessing the Internet, and Creating Shortcuts

Now that we have the basics of document and video creations; let's look at the Internet and what it has to offer. Here at left you see the icons of two of the most popular internet providers. These are snap shots of their individual Icons as seen on my "Computer Desktop".

You can access the internet by clicking on these from your desk top, or from your "Start Menu" where you will see your internet service provider's icon displayed as mine is here at right. At that point, simply double click on the icon to get started.

Creating Short-Cut Icons on Your Desktop...

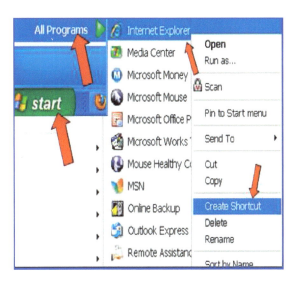

If you do not have an Internet Provider Icon on your desktop, here is how you can place one there.

First go to the "Start" button. Next you will click on "All Programs" to bring up a list of your computer's programs. From there you will look for, as example at left, the Internet Explorer tab. Next, you place your cursor over the tab and **right click** on the tab to bring up the drop down menu. From there you click "Create Shortcut." Now this shortcut will be automatically placed on your Desk Top.

Setting Up Your Internet Home Page (Introduction)...

If you do not have your internet set to open up on your desired "Home Page" when you click on the internet icon as explained above; you can create that setting by following the easy 1, 2, 3, & 4 steps described on the next two pages. Let's go there and take a look!

Navigating the Internet,
Setting Your Default Internet Provider & Home Page...

I am assuming that you already have your internet connection set up; and if so you will see your internet icons displayed either on your Desktop, or within the "Start Menu Panel" as explained on the previous page. Though your internet may be set up, you may not have your computer set to open the internet to your desired internet location; this is called the "Home Page." I like to open the internet to my desired home page instead of a provider's default page.

(Step 1) Accessing the Control Panel...
First you need to open your Control Panel which is displayed when you click on your "Start Button" as seen above to the right. This will open up the following "Control Panel" window shown here, and from this menu you click on "Network and Internet Connections".

(Step 2)
Accessing Your Internet Connections & Internet Options Settings...
From the "Network and Internet Connections" window, you click on "Internet Options" as seen below. When you click on the Internet Options window you will open the window shown below.

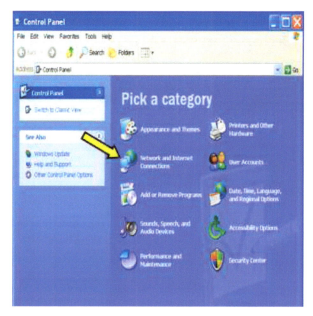

(Step 3)
Making Changes to Internet Connections & Internet Options Settings...

Now, let's proceed to the next page where we will have opened up our "Internet Properties" window. This is the window that appears after we clicked on the "Internet Options" menu selection shown at left. From the Internet Properties window we will designate our internet service provider and set our default internet home page. **Ready? Let's Go!**

(Step 4)
Designating Your Internet Provider Connection & Setting Your Default Home Page...

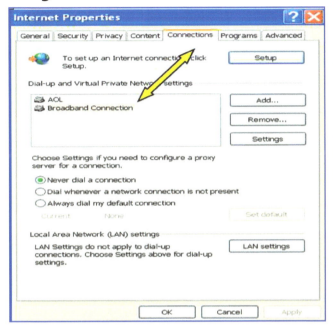

On the previous page, from the "Network and Internet Connections" window we clicked on the "Internet Options" tab to open this "Internet Properties" window at left which displays my current internet connections.

==Note, because my internet service is purchased through AOL and their broadband agreement with Verizon, my list shows two connections.==

The (Broadband Connection) is my preferred connection so I have highlighted that provider as shown.

Now, whenever I sign on to the internet I will be signing in with my Broadband Connection. When using a Broadband Connection, you should always have the "**Never dial a connection**" option tabbed to prevent your computer from attempting to dial up verses using your high speed internet.

Designating My Home Page...
By clicking on the "General" tab within this window I can type in where I want my home page to be. In this instance, since I use AOL, I have typed the AOL address as my "Home Page" destination. If you do not have a subscription such as AOL you should click on "Use blank" to open up on your default internet provider page, such as Internet Explorer, Mozilla Firefox, and so on. Note, you can name what ever destination you prefer, for instance it could be Google's search page.

You can easily do that by typing http://www.google.com in this location to open up your internet experience on that page.

Well, we have now covered the basics of setting your Internet's default settings. I think we are ready to get on line and use the things we have learned to explore the unlimited possibilities that the internet has to offer. **Let's Get Online! The Fun Begins!**

Understanding Your Internet Toolbar Functions

To navigate online it is important for you to understand your internet tool bar options and applications.   Tool bars vary according to the internet provider, so for your benefit we will look at two of the most common internet provider tool bars. When, you connect to the internet you will open up on your internet page containing your internet provider's toolbar at the top of the page. This is Mozilla Firefox's internet tool bar. Let's look at the features here.

Toolbar for Mozilla Firefox, Using the Search Bar to Navigate Internet Locations...

= The area marked with the green arrow is the "Internet Search Bar". If I want to go to another internet destination from the search bar you can simply place the cursor inside the search bar area and click the right mouse button once and then select the option "Select All" from the drop down menu to highlight that internet address as shown here at

right.   After you have highlighted the current address as shown, you can either press the "Backspace Key" on your keyboard to clear the field, or you can press the "Delete Key" to quickly delete the search bar field area.

Then, simply type a new internet address and press "Enter" to go to that destination from within this open window.

Note, it is not always necessary that you type (http://) before you type (www.) within an internet address; for the most part, using (www.) at the start of an internet destination point will get you there. Let's look at another internet navigational option on this toolbar.

= The blue arrows indicate the additional tabs I have open online. This means that I can have more that one online destination open as I explore the internet; although only one tab will be opened up in the online view window at a time. The online window currently opened will be that one displayed in the search bar field.

= Notice that I have several tabs open on my internet toolbar above.   The yellow arrow is pointing to a tab that shows a **+** sign. If I want to keep the opened tabs active, and yet open up another online destination tab, all I have to do is click on the **+** sign tab to open another internet destination window within the toolbar.

= This arrow is your "Go Back" button. By clicking on this button you can go back to the page you were on prior to your current location while in that internet tab's window. Remember, these are the basics that will give you a good platform to work form as you explore online. The button shown at right is the "Refresh Button", this button will refresh the page you are on if things seem to lock up, or don't function correctly.

Understanding Your Internet Toolbar Functions

Toolbar for Explorer, Using the Search Bar to Navigate Internet Locations...

= Just like with Mozilla Firefox, the area marked with the green arrow is the "Internet Search Bar". From here you type the internet destination you would like to visit.

= Though not marked with a **+** sign, this is your new tabs destination feature. By clicking on this tab you will open a new window where you can type your internet destination into that window's search bar field.

= This arrow is your "Go Back" button. By clicking on this button you can go back to the page you were on prior to your current location while in that internet tab's window. Note that if you go back you can also go forward by clicking on the right arrow which will take you to the previous window of your online search. Mozilla Firefox has this same option associated with its "Go Back" button.

= Just as in Mozilla Firefox, the blue arrows indicate the additional tabs I have open online. This means that I can have more that one online destination open as I explore the internet; although only one tab will be opened up in the view window pane at a time. The online window currently opened will be that one displayed in the search bar field.

Book Marking Favorite Sites...

= I wanted to talk a little about "Book Marking Your Favorite Sites". Just as when you are reading a book, and want to save the page location so you can come back to it; the internet provides this same type of application with the Book Mark, or Favorites' Feature. Bookmarks or Favorites' store your internet sites in a folder named as Book Mark or Favorites' depending on your internet provider.

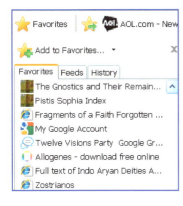

Here is an example... Let's say you are on a web page that you really like a lot, and you want to be able to visit that site again. Instead of having to write down the entire website address, you can simply click on the favorites as tab shown above. Clicking on that button, (above right), will open up the drop down menu, (at left), which lists my current favorite sites. If you want to add the site you are currently, simply click on the "Add to Favorites" option to have that site added to your list of favorite websites. Next time you want to visit there, just click Favorites and you will find it listed there.

How to Upload a Video to YouTube

Now that we have learned the basics of navigating the internet; I think it is time that we upload our video we created to YouTube for everyone to enjoy...!

Before you can upload a YouTube video you must create a User's Account...

Let's get started Creating a User's Account on YouTube...

As you can see here at left, I have my internet window opened to the YouTube internet site where I want to "Upload" my video to YouTube. However, if I do not have an account with YouTube already, when I click the upload option (blue arrow); instead, I will be taken to a pop-up window that suggests that I create a YouTube Account.

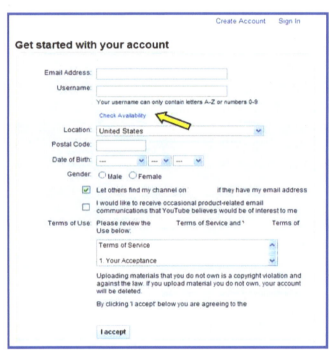

You can create your own account if you click on the "Create Account" option shown above (red arrow). So let's create our YouTube Account Now! After clicking on the "Create Account" option, you will be taken to this create an account page shown at left where you will complete the information and then click the "I Accept" button to initiate the creation of your YouTube Account.

Note: I have whitened out the names of the pertinent companies in the Terms of Use and Acceptance contractual areas so as to avoid any infringements to their contracts copy writes or registered trademarks.

Hint:
When filling out this form, to save yourself some time, before you click on the "I accept" button use the, "Check Availability" link shown with the (yellow arrow) to be certain your desired user name is not being used by another. If so, you will have to select another user name to proceed with establishing your YouTube account. When you have completed this form and clicked "Accept" to establish your user's account, you can simply go to the YouTube Website, sign in to your account and begin to upload your videos as described on the next page.

So let's go to the next page and learn about how to upload our video to YouTube!

How to Upload a Video to YouTube

On the previous page we discussed how to set up your YouTube Account. Now that you have your account established you will be able to upload videos to YouTube from your computer's video files; or from another location within YouTube itself, or another website provided you have the embedding code.

Starting Your Video Upload...
The first thing you need to know with regard to uploading a video on YouTube is that the video must not be longer than 15 minutes. So when you are ready to upload your video, these are the steps you need to follow.

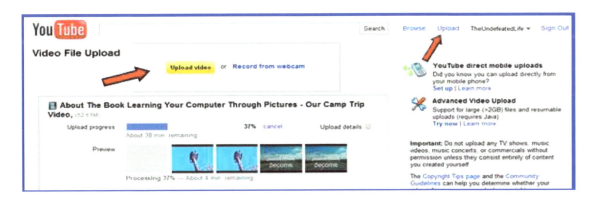

Step One: If you are going to upload from your computer's video files then you click on the "Upload" options shown here at left, (red arrows). This will open either your video file itself, shown lower left, or your documents folder, shown lower right. In each of these upload options you will need to highlight the video file you want to upload and then click "Open" to begin YouTube's upload process.

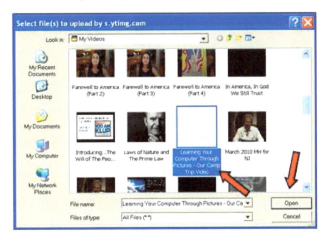

O.K. now we are ready to go to the next page and discuss the upload window that you will be working in after you have clicked on the "Open" button to begin the process.

How to Upload a Video to YouTube

Step Two:

Now this window has opened which has begun the process of uploading our video, let's look at what we need to do here...

The (yellow) arrows show the progress of our upload.

The (red arrow) is where you type in the name of your video. Note: when this process begins there will be an ending that indicates the type of file being uploaded, e.g. (.WAV); I recommend that you remove this ending so that your video title looks more natural to its content.

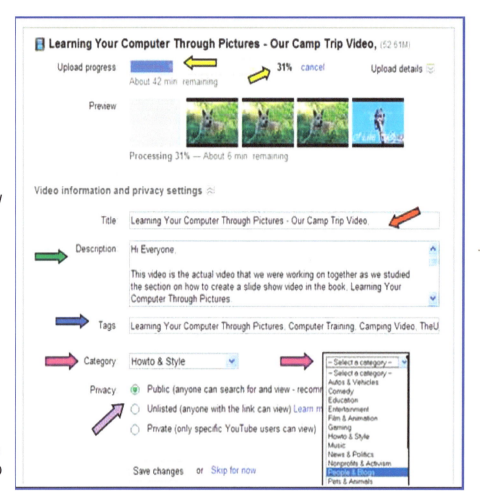

The (green arrow) indicates your description field. In other words, you need to describe this video and its purpose. Try to make this description as personal and entertaining as possible so that people will be interested in its content.

The (blue arrow) is very important. These tags are "Search Engine Key Words", meaning that when someone types one of these words in a search engine, whether on YouTube or somewhere else, your video is likely to appear in that search. Notice that I have included the title of the book related to this video.

The (pink arrows) indicates the category that this video will be placed on in YouTube's directory of video content listings. For personal usage, the "People & Blogs" (insert at right) is the common category that most people use.

The (purple arrow) shows that under the "Privacy" settings, I have selected "Public" as I want everyone to be able to view this video. The other settings pertaining to privacy are self explanatory. After you have completed these fields, you simply click on the "Save Changes" button to complete the process.

How to Upload a Video to YouTube

Step Three:

Getting Your Video's URL & Embedding Codes...

O.K. now your video is finished uploading, and in the upload window, at the bottom of the pane you will see that YouTube has given your video its specific "URL", the location on the internet that it can be found, and also you have been given what is called an "Embed Code." This code can be copied and pasted onto other internet sites or pages as a video player so that people can watch your video from the location you place this code.

To grab this code and place it somewhere else you first place your cursor within the Embed field of this window. Then you right click with your mouse in this location and select copy from the drop down menu. After you have copied this code you can place it somewhere else so that people can watch the video without having to go to YouTube. I like to use this feature in blogs, or on other websites. It is a great way to get your ideas across in a very entertaining and visual manner.

Success!
When YouTube has finished your video upload you will get this message...

About Auto Share...
You will see this window option from YouTube which allows you to share your video on your other online social media networks. To do that read the instructions at right.

How to Upload a Video to YouTube

About Upload Details...

A quick note about your video's "Upload Details". If you click on the tab shown at right for Upload details, you will open the drop down information pane shown here. This pane gives you the specifics about your video.

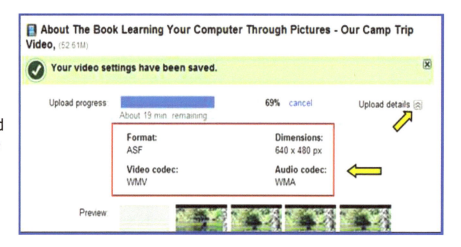

Finding Your YouTube Videos within Your YouTube Channel Account...

At the bottom of the "Upload Video" page, you will see the box shown above. Notice the words, "My videos", (red arrow)? If you want to see the other videos stored in your YouTube account's Channel, clicking on this tab will open up the following window as shown below. Here you can see all of your videos that have been uploaded on your YouTube channel. Notice that the current upload is indicated as, "Upload (processing please wait), (green arrow).

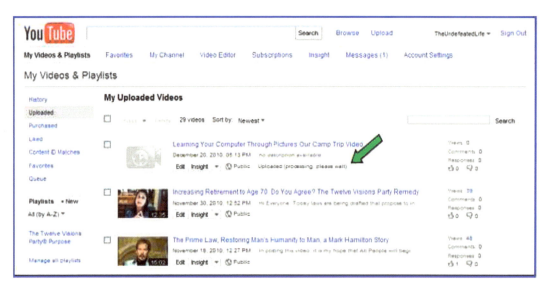

How to Upload a Video to YouTube, Using Your Web Camera

Step One:

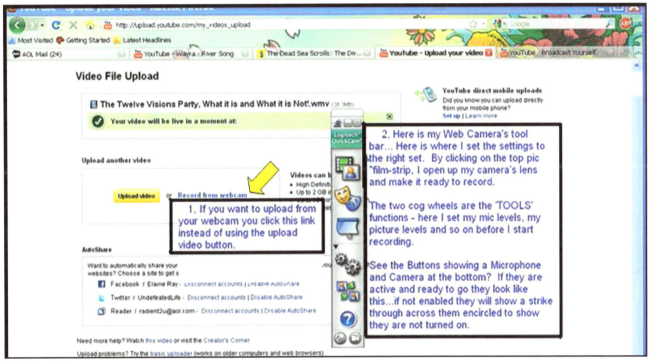

Step Two:

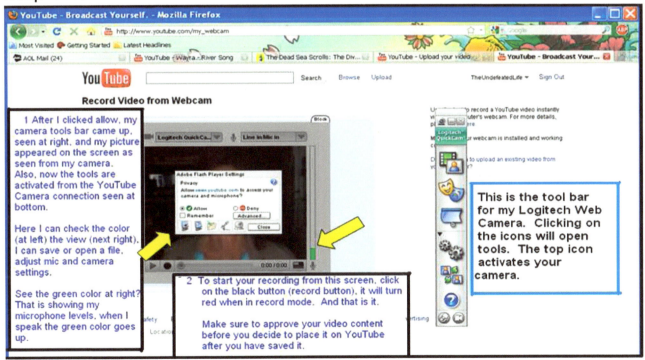

Final Notes on "How to Upload a YouTube Video"

Well that concludes our lessons...
Congratulations on your accomplishments in working these basics on understanding your computer as presented.

You can view the video we created in our tutorial on my YouTube Channel by clicking on this link: http://www.youtube.com/watch?v=yLN0gjWZr6M

~ Conclusion ~

I hope you have enjoyed this study guide on, "Learning Your Computers Through Pictures." Oh, one more thing...

Throughout this book you have seen a picture of this dog sleeping, and the question, "Why is this dog sleeping?"   Well, have you figured it out?

Congratulations, it is because this dog is no longer using the computer...You Are!!!

Thank you for purchasing this book....

Elaine Ray

P.S. You can order copies of this book for your friends, or contact me on the contact page by going to: http://www.theundefeatedlife.com

About the Author

Elaine Ray worked for the Los Angeles County Education Department, Special Education Division for 10 years as an Assistant Special Education Instructor.

Her primary focus in this field was using augmentative communications technology to assist functionally mute children with their language development. She states that understanding how precious our ability to communicate is; and knowing that the technology is out there that can facilitate our communicative needs, was a great influencer in her development of the Learning Your Computer Through Pictures tool.

The passing of her Father, and familial hardships caused her to drop out of high school at an early age; nevertheless, she went on to graduate from Shasta Bible College with honors, receiving her A.A. Degree in General Education. She then went on to receive her B.A. Degree in Special Education from Alameda University.

Elaine states, "With clear and concise instructions anybody can do just about anything." Elaine hopes that everyone will enjoy the skills and accomplishments they receive from working through this basic computer applications workbook. You can learn more about Elaine by visiting her website at:
www.theundefeatedlife.com